Falling In Love God's Way

By A. R. Neal

Precious Media Group Atlanta, Georgia

All rights reserved. This book, or parts thereof, may not be reproduced in any form or by any means, electronic or mechanical without permission in writing from the publisher.

Copyright © 2011 by A. R. Neal

A. R. Neal

For more information about
the writing of the author, visit
www.fallinginlovegodsway.org

Acknowledgements

There is so much involved where God is taking me and God is doing it in His time. I am grateful for favor that God has given through many of my friends and associates.

To my wife, thank you for showing me unconditional love and unusual kindness. I will always treasure our love. You motivate and inspire me to reach the highest level of my potential. Mere words cannot describe the wife and woman of God you are. I thank God for blessing us as we are together. I will always love you.

To my mother, Ruby Neal, there is no me without you. Writing is in my blood and it began with you. Thank you for teaching me morals and values. I love you with all my heart.

To two special people in my life, my daughter Maranda, and my son Jason. I love and thank God for both of you.

To my sister D. Elaine McNease, who has been an inspiration all my life. Thank you for the encouragement, love, and correction. Thank you for being motherly when necessary. Thank you for being my best friend and sister. I appreciate your support, assistance, and tireless dedication on this book. I truly love you.

To Pastor Jamelle Mckenzie, I thank you for always being supportive. God blessed me with a true friend, pastor, and sister. You have been a great blessing to me. Although we are not biologically related we are one in Christ. I love you woman of God.

To Myrthia Hall, thank you for believing in me. I appreciate your encouragement and continual support. God bless.

To Suzan Jackson, thank you so much for your patience in software training, editing, and publishing; to Jeremiah Lamb, web design and video productions; Pastor Michael Dennis, video productions, cover design, audio productions, and computor training; Mona Scott (author), inspiration and encouragement; Richard Evans, cover design;

Angela Butler for the blog radio interview; Laura McClary for always motivating me; Cynthia Williams a Support Coordinator for South Carolina; Kfend Alpha for logos for FILGW and GWIOM, Clive and Marva Mckenzie for spiritual and financial support, and I thank God in advance for all others who God will send that will aide in the seminars and workshops that FILGW will host.

Thanks again and I don't take any acts of kindness for granted.

Contents

Preface	i
Introduction	v
Chapter 1: Understanding God's Love	1
Chapter 2: Know Yourself	14
Chapter 3: Let Go Let God	20
Chapter 4: What Does God See In Your Mate?	31
Chapter 5: Entwined	39
Chapter 6: My Supposed To Be	52
Chapter 7: Don't Stop Climbing The Mountain	66
Chapter 8: Till Death Do We Part	90
Afterward	110
Notes	112
About the Author	113

Preface

The first day that I interacted with Precious, I knew in my spirit that we would be entwined with God and each other. We always told everyone that we were introduced by a mutual friend. The friend that we were talking about was God. We felt that was all anyone needed to know.

I remember the first night that I tried calling her. It was October 8, 2010 at 8:30 p.m. She asked me to call her cell phone but the line was continually busy. I also tried her home number with the same results. I reluctantly called my sister to see if she could call from her phone. My sister called and got the same results. Finally I began to pray and the next time I called her the line was clear.

I knew then that our relationship was going to be special. Satan did not want us to talk. Little did I know that prayer would be the basis of our relationship. Our first conversation was informative, peaceful, and comforting. I knew that she was in ministry, but she was not aware that I was a minister. The first question she asked me was, "Do you know how to pray?" As we were about to say good night, after talking about five hours, she calmly said, "You can pray now." I laughed softly to myself because I knew what she was doing. Precious was testing me to see what type of prayer life I had. In this way, she could summarize my relationship with God. At the time I was not aware that she was an intercessor.

Well, that night God revealed to me that this was the woman He had given me. God revealed things to me about her that even amazed her. We were in different states, but seemed so close.

Although things happened so rapidly, we knew instantly that we were each other's *supposed to be*. God put in my spirit before we married to write a book about our relationship and marriage. We wanted to have a godly model relationship and marriage; therefore, we realized that we had to live accordingly. As a result, this would be an anointed book; for this reason, the title *Falling In Love God's Way*, was conceived and birthed by God.

Introduction

Falling In Love God's Way

In my opinion, most have not experienced the ecstasy of having a true loving experience. Most of the time there is an endless search to fill an evasive void. Perhaps this search completes one's inward need to have a loving companionship and marriage.

God chose me as the recipient of a life changing experience. This is the result of an answered prayer. For example, this prayer preceded preparation, testing, and confirmation. For this reason, the love story of **Precious** and **Neal** is amazing. Therefore, after hearing the story, most of the responses were, "it sounds like a fairy tale."

Many people call Precious Bougrine Neal an

angel of God. In fact, our union is heavenly. Because of this, God's power and presence fills every brief moment we spend together.

Our initial conversation was on the telephone. After talking a few minutes I will never forget her asking, "Can you pray?" I often smile when I think about that question. When she asked, I had not told her that I was in ministry. I immediately recognized that she was unique and highly anointed.

Precious made it perfectly clear what she wanted and she trusted God to bless her with the desires of her heart. For one thing Precious expressed her desire for a husband. Another thing she prayed for was a husband she could "love whole-heartedly," and receive the same in return. She adamantly told me that she did not date because "that would leave room for Satan to overtake your weaknesses."

Yes, I wondered how one could get to know a person without dating. Well, I learned from her that when one meets her or his spirit mate, not soul mate, then she or he is directly connected to God which will entwine the relationship with God.

I realized the second night that we talked God had given me my wife, my *supposed to be*, and spirit mate. We met October 8, 2010 and married on November 27, 2010. She is a perfect Christian, mother, and wife.

It is a beautiful thing to fall in love. True love is not exasperating; it does not bring grief, is not irritating, or annoying. So many people have experienced what is initially thought of as love, only to find out that it was more of an illusion than anything else; the person begins emotionally and physically charged, and do not see any negative or red flags. What is more, the person focuses solely on what she or he wants to perceive; there is nothing anyone can tell that person, other than what she or he wants to hear.

In most cases, the meeting and dating experience begins with the attraction of a person's exterior or physical appearance. Rarely does a person begin with one's inner beauty. An outer attraction diminishes the foundation of a relationship. Therefore, it is not a good idea to consider physical appearance alone.

The outside is just a shell. Despite one's outside appearance there will always be someone interested. What is beautiful to one person is totally different to another, but there is someone for everyone (everyone defines beauty differently).

Eye candy is a description given when speaking about someone with good looks. For instance, I met a beautiful and nicely built young lady who, in spite of her beauty, annoyed me because she was a ding bell. Even though she was a teacher and highly educated, I was unable to connect with her. While I mentally tried my best, my physical body would not respond.

Needless to say, I learned two lessons from that experience. One, fornication does not show a godly relationship. Two, everything that looks good is not good for you.

Of course, I was in the world at that time. In

other words, **"worldly"** affairs. A godly spiritual behavior was not important to me at that time.

These lessons also helped me to understand the difference between the wisdom of God and the foolishness of " **worldly"** wisdom.

It is important to look at the heart, because it is the part of a person that is not physically seen, but it speaks the loudest and clearest.

The heart reveals the true character of a person. *Proverbs 23:7* tells us, *"As he thinketh in his heart so is he."* What is on the inside of a person will come out verbally or physically. It is up to each person not to be so consumed by outer appearances that she or he ignores another person's heart. Unfortunately, when the heart is not examined we leave room for disaster.

I have received a deeper revelation that will help a person make better choices when choosing a mate. Specifically, one must understand what to look for in a mate when pursuing a relationship in a godly fashion. If one searches to find God in a person's most inner being, then deception would not be so easy when discerning a person's character. In this way, the finished work is in progress and one can see the Spirit of God.

So many relationships and marriages become stagnate because of sexual escapades that include premarital sex.

The Bible tells us, *"It is good for a man not to touch a woman and avoid fornication" (1 Cor 7:1-2).*

The Greek word for touch in *1 Cor 7:1* is haptō which means, "to have carnal intercourse with a woman" (*Vine's Expository Dictionary of Old and New Testament Words, P. 638*). The Apostle Paul shows how important it is for a man and a woman not to become physically attached, this could lead to touching and ultimately sexual immorality. Therefore, his instructions in *1 Cor 7:2 is* to, *"avoid fornication by every man having his own wife, and every woman having her own husband."*

Based on my experience as a pastor, providing premarital counseling, most couples are overly concerned about sexual gratification from and by their mate. In other words they are curious as to whether they will meet each other's sexual expectations in bed.

Likewise, when Precious and I began planning our matrimonial ceremony, I admit there was a concern; in particular, I questioned her about sex. Her response led me to believe that she could fulfill all my needs intimately.

We never tested the waters, but chose to trust God that it would be overwhelming. Without saying too much, I must admit she is the best lover I have ever had.

Our romance was like a whirlwind and the wind was the Holy Spirit. I will not say that unions like ours does not happen, but I will say that most people do not allow it to happen supernaturally.

God positioned us individually so that we would be ready to receive His blessing. Prior to meeting Precious, I had totally submitted my spirit, body, and mind to God. Indeed, to receive a highly anointed woman of God, I had to be at a certain place in my walk with God. Yes, things happened so quickly.

I shared the news of my new-found love with only a couple of people, Jamelle Mckenzie, my pastor, and Delores McNease, my sister. Of course, they are my accountability partners. Therefore, I knew they would understand this supernatural union.

Precious and I had a swift courtship. Although we were separated by states we were united in spirit. I lived in Georgia and she lived in Texas.

I did visit her for one week and we did not fornicate. Nevertheless, we were still tempted. This was extremely difficult since we knew God had already spoken to us and had ordained our union.

Through my ability to resist sexual sin, I learned that Precious had a greater respect for me. As men, we should never forget that we are the covering for our women. The covering does not begin after the marriage, but during the dating process.

Women should understand that men are not only the physical covering, but more so a spiritual covering. For this purpose, it is important to cover her with the strength of God, prayer, righteousness, patience, and love.

When a woman sees the man walking as her covering, the man will notice a godly submission that stimulates him to continue walking in his calling as a husband.

Although divorce rates are continually soaring, when God is in charge of a union, divorce becomes an unlikely choice or occurrence.

In his article, *Divorce and Remarriage, U.S. Divorce Rates for Various Faith Groups, Age Groups, & Geographic Areas,* B.A. Robinson shows a study done by Barna Research Group a few years ago; according to this study, *"50% of American marriages end in divorce, 11% of the adult population was divorced at that time and 25% of the adult population has experienced at least one divorce during their lifetime."*

The study also went on to illustrate the

percentages for Christian faith groups who have been divorced were as follows:

Non-denominational	34%
Baptist	29%
Mainline Protestants	25%
Mormons	24%
Catholics	21%
Lutherans	21% [1]

Donald Hughes, author of *The Divorce Reality* stated, *"In churches, people have a superstitious view that Christianity will keep them from divorce, but they are subject to the same problems as everyone else, and they include a lack of relationship skills. Just being born again is a rabbit's foot."* Hughes claims that *"90% of divorces among born-again couples occur after they have been saved."* [2]

Hughes has some interesting points of view but, I think it's a very general statement. All Christians are not on the same level. Some are simply babes in Christ. Of course, storms do not bypass anyone and everyone will experience a test at some point.

Moreover, being born again represents more than a rabbit's foot; it is a lifestyle.

Now let us view the percentage of those who have been divorced (*given by Barna Research Group*) based on religion. Barna reports the following:

Jews	*30%*
Born-Again Christians	*27%*
Christians	*42%*
Atheists, Agnostics	*21%*

The divorce rate for Atheists and Agnostics is lower than any other religious groups. This does not mean the answer is to not be a Christian, but a decision must be made based on righteous principals and morals.

The Bible speaks about divorce in several Scriptures. One example is *Matthew 19:6*, which states, "Wherefore they are no more twain, but one flesh. What therefore God hath joined together, let not man put asunder." So many divorces occur because of the lack of oneness and because God has not ordained the marriage. In other words, this Scripture shows why a couple should not divorce. So many divorces occur because of the lack of oneness and because God did not ordain the marriage.

In particular, when two people live in oneness, it means that they are living in one accord. When one spouse hurts, the other one hurts. Precious and I always say to each other, "I'm you and you are me; we are one."

When God truly joins a marriage, it will be eternal. Satan is always busy trying to kill, steal, and destroy. He is not pleased with spirit-filled, loving, or unified marriages.

When counseling couples, I tell them in our first meeting that at the end of our sessions I will recommend them to marry or wait. There have been couples who were not happy with my decision not to marry them, but I feel confident in my decisions in those cases, because too many marriages fail because they were not ordained by God.

Chapter 1

The gift of love is magnified when it is received without hesitation or discord.

Understanding God's Love

Everything begins with our Father. The Bible states, *"I am Alpha and Omega, the beginning and the end"* (*Rev 22:13*). God is love; in particular, *"For God so loved the world, that He gave His only begotten Son, that whosoever believeth in Him should not perish, but have everlasting life"* (*Jn 3:16*). God loved His creation so much that He wanted the best for people. God wanted redemption and His people set free, so that one day God's people could be with Him. So what does God do? God gives!

Love is not love without sharing. One can say to another, "I love you," but it is more than mere talk. Love is a verb; love is an action word. One shows love by the way she or he treats and responds to others. God showed His love by giving people an important part of Him, which reflects who God is.

God's gift was further magnified by the fact that we, as Christians, became heirs and *"joint heirs with Christ"* (*Rom 8 :17*). Then Christ being so much like His Father, gave us an unforgettable gift, His life!

Abraham showed this same type of love when he was willing to offer his own son Isaac as a sacrifice. He loved God so much that without pondering or doubting, he was willing to give his son of promise *(Gen 22:1-9)*. Sometimes, God will test people to see if they love Him more than anything or anyone.

The gift of love magnifies when one expresses it without hesitation or discord. As an example, Ruth showed how much she loved Naomi when she sacrificed her life in Moab while staying with her mother-in-law in Bethlehem (*Ruth* 1:19).

Unfortunately, many people do not know how to accept something that is so genuine, pure, and unconditional. One of the most disheartening feelings is giving or sharing love, and as a result experience rejection. God's love is so awesome, yet so unappreciated by many.

Often times when dating, some people misinterpret what they think love is for what true love really is. Furthermore, mixed signals are given and received usually because one person is seeking something totally different from the other. Consequently, this creates disharmony in the relationship.

When dating, it is important to know in the beginning what each person expects from the other, and be willing to meet those expectations if they are godly.

When falling in love God's way, one's attitude and actions should show God's presence. When God's love exists in a person's heart, it shows in that person's actions.

One way of describing love is having an intense affection for another based on familiar or personal ties. Sometimes physical or emotional attraction causes one to believe that she or he is in love.

On the contrary, God's love is vastly different from people's love. The physical and emotional attraction that one may call love is conditional, mercurial, and fickled.

I experienced this type of love when my ex-wife told me she had, "fallen out of love with me." She stated, "We have grown apart." I felt that the marriage vows we pledged "for better or worse, for richer or poorer, through sickness and health, till death do us part," meant very little. As was the case in my marriage, and I also believe that to so many others, "till death" really means "till death of love" do we part and not a partner's physical death.

A feeling of love for most people is definitely conditional and it is usually based on something. In other words, some people say, "I love you because..." We could fill in the blank with "what you have, how you look, how you make me feel, or who you are." Furthermore, this establishes the need for unconditional love.

Warren W. Wiersbe, the author of *On Being A*

Servant Of God wrote, *"After all, it is an awesome thing to be God's servant and do His will. Like marriage, Christian service should not be entered into lightly or carelessly, but reverently, soberly and in the fear of God."* Wiersbe also states from *The Book of Common Prayer* that, *"finding unconditional love in any friendship, relationship, or marriage is often very difficult."*[3]

The love parents have for their children is as close to unconditional love that one can experience without the help of God's love. Parents love their children through good and bad times. It does not matter what anyone says or thinks. Parental love never changes. However, more than parental love, God's love transcends all human love. In order to know true love one must receive God's love. God wants to pour out His love on people. God wants to teach people how to love others as He loves. The greatest description of love is given in *1 Corinthians 13:1-13*:

If I [can] speak in the tongues of men and [even] of angels, but have not love (that reasoning, intentional, spiritual devotion such as is inspired by God's love for and in us), I am only a noisy gong or a clanging cymbal. And if I have prophetic powers (the gift of interpreting the divine will and purpose), and understand all the secret truths and mysteries and possess all knowledge, and if I have [sufficient] faith so that I can remove mountains, but have not love (God's love in me) I am nothing (a useless nobody). Even if I dole out all that I have [to the poor in providing] food, and if I surrender my body to be burned or in order that I may glory, but have not love (God's love in me), I gain nothing. Love endures long and is patient and kind; love is never envious nor boils over with jealously; is not boastful or vainglorious; does not display itself haughtily. It is not conceited (arrogant and inflated with pride); it is not rude (unmannerly) and does not act unbecomingly. Love (God's love in us) does not insist on its own rights or its own way, for it is not self-seeking; it is not touchy or fretful or resentful; it takes no account of the evil done to it [it pays no attention to a suffered wrong]. It does not rejoice at injustice and unrighteousness, but *rejoices when right and truth prevail. Love bears up under anything and everything that comes; is ever ready to believe the best of every person, its hopes are fadeless under all circumstances, and it endures everything [without weakening] Love never fails [never fades out or becomes obsolete or comes to an end]. As for prophecy (the gift of interpreting the divine will and purpose), it will be fulfilled and pass away; as for tongues, they will cease; as for knowledge, it will pass away [it will lose its value and be superseded by truth]. For our knowledge is fragmentary (incomplete and imperfect). But when the complete and perfect (total) comes, the incomplete and imperfect will vanish away (become antiquated, void, and superseded). When I was a child, I talked like a child, I thought like a child, I reasoned like a child; now that I have become a man, I am done with childish ways and have put them aside. For now we are looking in a mirror that gives only a dim (blurred) reflection [of reality as in a riddle or enigma], but then [when perfection comes] we shall see in reality and face to face! Now I know in part (imperfectly), but then I shall know and understand fully and clearly, even in the same manner as I have been fully and clearly known and understood [by God]. And so faith, hope, love abide [faith, conviction and belief respecting man's relation to God and divine things; hope, joyful and confident expectation of eternal salvation; love, true affection for God and man, growing out of God's love for and in us], these three; but the greatest of these is love (Amplified).*

One can experience a transforming effect in life if the soul and spirit is saturated with this Scripture. As previously mentioned in the introduction, "True love is not exasperating, it does not bring grief, it is not irritating, or annoying." Of course, true love is godly. Some of the descriptions of love in 1 *Cor 13*, which was quoted earlier in this chapter, is an example of a godly love. Indeed, this is agape love (which will be explained in this chapter). Many times people get involved in loves other than agape such as, eros, philia, storge, and thelema.

The most dominate love that the world displays is eros. Eros is passionate love with sensual desire and longing. The Modern Greek word erotas means romantic love. However, eros does not have to be sexual. Eros can be interpreted as a love for someone whom a person may have more than the love of friendship. It can also apply to dating relationships as well as marriages. Although eros is initially felt for a person with contemplation, it becomes an appreciation of beauty within that person, or becomes an appreciation of beauty itself.

A second type of love that we share is philia. Philia means friendship in Modern Greek. A dispassionate virtuous love, this type of love was a concept developed by Aristotle. It includes loyalty to friends, family, and community. It requires virtue, equality, and familiarity.

In ancient texts, philia denoted the general type of love and is used to describe the love between family, friends, or a desire or enjoyment of an activity (as well as between lovers). This part may sound confusing because of a previous statement implying that phila is not classified for lovers.

Consequently, this is the only other word for love used in the ancient text of the New Testament apart from agape, but it is used less frequently.

Agape is the third type of love that when received and given, should grab the heart of each individual that desires to truly experience the presence, power, freedom, and joy of God's love.

Agape is unconditional; it releases strongholds and also exemplifies the meaning of how we should express our love for one another. Furthermore, agape means love in modern day Greek; in ancient Greek, it often refers to general affection rather than affection suggested by eros. Additionally, agape is used in ancient texts to denote feelings for a good meal, one's children, or the feelings for a spouse. What is more, agape is the feeling of being content or holding another in high regard.

The verb appears in the New Testament when the relationship between Jesus and the beloved disciple John is described (*Jn* 20:2). In biblical literature its meaning and usage is illustrated by self-sacrifice, and giving love to all, both friend and enemy.

Agape is also used in *Matthew 22:39* which states, *"Thou shalt love thy neighbor as thyself,"* or as *John 15:12* states, *"This is my commandment, that* ye *love one another, as I have loved you,"* and *1 John 4:8* tells us, *"He that loveth not knoweth not God; for God is love."*

On the other hand, the word agape is not always used in a positive sense. The Apostle Paul writes in *2 Timothy 4:10, "For Demas hath forsaken me having loved (agapo) this present world."* Thus the word agape is not always used of a divine love or the love of God. Demas was one of Paul's co-laborers who abandoned him for the love of the world.

Storge, a fourth type of love means "affection" in Modern Greek. It is a natural affection like that felt by parents for their children. Storge is rarely used in ancient works and then almost exclusively as a description of relationship among family members.

The fifth and last type of love being described is

thelema, which means "desire" in Modern Greek. It is the desire to do something, to be occupied, to be in preeminence.

It is important to understand and recognize the different types of love. Personally, I strive to walk daily in agape love. When a person allows agape love to saturate and penetrate her or his most inner being that love will flow out of the heart.

Indeed, that flow becomes an overflow that encompasses all of the other types of love. In other words, each type of love is put in its proper place. Eros' sensual desires, philia's loyalty to friends, family, and community, storge's natural affection for family, and thelema's desire for fulfillment will not overtake God's agape unconditional love!

Prayer

Father, I pray in the name of Jesus that we learn how to walk in your unconditional love. I pray that relationships and marriages are drenched with agape love. I rebuke selfishness, contention, hatred, and strife. Teach us how to love one another. I thank you that we will walk in your unconditional love and it reflects the way we treat one another. In Jesus' name I pray. Amen.

Chapter 2

> *There are those who are wandering in the desert of loneliness because the part of them that remains unknown is the missing link to who they are.*

Know Yourself

Many would ask, "What does knowing yourself have to do with falling in love God's way?" The first stage of communication between interested parties consist of questions and answers. Initial conversations are times of openness and truthfulness that shows the heart of both parties involved.

The word of God tells us, *"Let a man examine himself"* (1 Cor 11:28). This particular Scripture references partaking of the Lord's Supper. It is important for one to look inwardly before committing to accept, believe, and live whole-heartedly for our Lord and Savior. God expects honesty within people and with Him.

Everyone should examine themselves before getting involved in a relationship. In particular, one should consider and deal with any personal, unresolved issues. These issues may consist of a number of things such as, drinking problems, drugs, an uncontrollable temper, or abuse.

Sharing these issues early in the relationship shows honesty and reflects how one sees her or his mate throughout the relationship. No matter what the issue is now or was before the relationship began, it is important to share these details. Moreover, concealing these issues could lead to consequences later. In this way, a person shows honesty with one's self and it reflects how others see this person.

For many, looking inward is difficult. In *Matthew 7:3* Jesus asks, *"why beholdest thou the mote that is in thy brother's eye, but considerest not the beam that is in thine own eye?"* He was teaching on not judging others and being hypocritical. How can I love someone properly if I act perfect or self-righteous? I always mention my unworthiness of having such a wife who is a woman of God and truly walks in agape love.

When I am out-of-order and self-righteous, I ask her forgiveness. There are times when it is necessary for a person to dissect unrighteousness and ugliness from within. This enables one to say "I'm sorry." It also gives one the opportunity to ask for forgiveness before being confronted.

I realize that sometimes I am unintentionally abrasive, impatient, and blunt. However, I am continually striving to improve my demeanor in those areas. There are times that I expect people to respond the same way I would. That is not always good although my way may seem right. The key is learning to meet others where they are.

In Chapter 4, the topic, *What Does God See In Your Mate*, deals with how God looks at each one of us. Knowing who we are is how we intimately look at ourselves. The Apostle Paul even examined himself when he said in *Romans 7:24, "O wretched man that I am!"* He also encourages us not to think that we are all that or already where we should be.

God made each one of us differently; for this reason, a DNA or finger prints uniquely identifies each person. One may look, talk, or act like another person, but a person can never exchange, borrow, or match someone's DNA. For instance, many people who commit crimes are convicted because of their genetic identity.

In addition, God gave us a soul, will, emotions, and intellect. In essence, we are spirit, body, and soul. Our spirit is where God is and that is where He wants us to live. It is from the dust of the ground that God breathed in man the breath of life; His Spirit, and man became a living soul.

The question is who are you? Are you the person who feels that one's status determines her or his occupation, income, physical appearance, or social status?

The concern for many couples are their outer characteristics and not the inner part of their being. Relationships often fail because people portray or highlight their most dominant attributes. They expose the thing or things that makes them look attractive or arresting. Knowing one's self is realizing that one aspect of a person's character or status does not determine who the person really is!

Some people are wandering in the desert of loneliness because one part of that person remains unknown. Surely, that part is the missing link of who that person really is. Therefore, one must unveil the true self to receive her or his God sent mate. Otherwise, the opportunity or the experience may never happen.

One of the most important reasons for me knowing myself is, my wife becomes me and I will become her. We were so equally yoked from the beginning of our relationship that we began saying, "I am you and you are me!"

Although our personalities are different we are

so alike. For this reason, I hear her always saying, "I am you honey." Well, she could never have been me if I had not discovered who I was. Let us always be mindful that the "you" that your mate becomes shows in the treatments you receive. What is more, the likeness shared goes farther than having the same last name. Precious is who I am in Christ, honesty, love, commitment, and morally. In the same way, I am who Precious is.

Prayer

I thank you Lord for your presence in my life. Lord let me continually examine myself and please forgive me for failing You with unholy attitudes, unrighteousness, and abrasiveness. God, I pray that you make me whole and fix those areas that are lacking in my character and my walk with you. Thank you Lord, in Jesus' name I pray. Amen.

Chapter 3

Timing is everything, God's timing is supreme. It can be the difference between receiving an awaited blessing and striving a longer period to receive it.

Let Go Let God

"In the beginning was the Word and the Word was with God, and the Word was God" (Jn 1:1)."The Word became flesh and dwelt among us" (Jn 4:1). This Scripture establishes that God is the beginning of all things and that Jesus was with Him.

The blessing for all people is that *Jesus became flesh and dwelt among us*. The *Word* became alive; something that Christians can personally identify with. Jesus taught about life, love, marriage, and sin.

Jesus left a standard so high that many use the

acronym, WWJD ("What Would Jesus Do?") Every action or decision that one makes should confirm Jesus' teachings. *"We have not a high priest that cannot be touched with the feelings of our infirmities, but was in all points tempted like or as we are, yet without sin"* (*Heb 4:15*). That releases us from doing it our way to simply following God's plan for our lives.

Timing is everything, God's timing is supreme. It can be the difference between receiving an awaited blessing and striving a longer period to receive the blessing.

When a person hesitates to move or listen when God speaks, this could affect the lives of others. This does not mean that the things God had planned will not happen, but ignoring God could hinder the original plan and cause a delay.

When a person learns to listen to that gentle small voice that speaks to her or his spirit, it becomes paramount. What is more, not only does the size of that person's blessings increase, but also the blessings of others. What a person does not hear can hinder or stagnate what God wants to do for someone else, but it will not stop it from happening!

When I met Precious I was not particularly looking for a mate. So many things were transpiring spiritually in my life at that time, dating was not a priority on my list. As a matter of fact, I was experiencing a transformation. At some point in a person's life there comes a time of self-evaluation. Up to this point everything basically was all about me!

I once heard someone say, "If you keep doing what you've been doing, you keep getting what you've been getting." The type of women I was getting would be thought of by many as, "the cream of the crop."

Glenda Lock, my childhood friend, told me that I needed to leave those controlling white-collar women alone, because they didn't really care about me. It would often appear that those were the type of women I pursued, but that was not true. My previous dating experience was a preparation for what God had waiting for me.

In the premarital stage so many get involved in what I call a love trap. In a love trap people simply settle for what they have, without really experiencing what God has for them. Why would anyone continue being lied to, cheated on, physically abused, and mistrusted without abandoning the relationship? Many would say, it is low self-esteem or insecurity. The love trap will try to make one feel as if a person's dependency is in a man or woman. The devil is a liar, we must truly learn how to follow and trust God in our lives and relationships.

I am not proud of many things I experienced in some of my relationship. Granted if I had not gone through some of these things, then others could not benefit and grow.

The last long-term relationship that I was in before Precious and I married is not one that I am proud of. It is not because she was not a good woman, but because I was totally out of God's order.

No doubt, the carnal part of me enjoyed the relationship. We traveled, laughed, and talked. We were even engaged to marry. This woman treated me like no other woman had. She washed and ironed my clothes, and she also bought clothes and cologne for me. I mentioned to her how much I liked the Chrysler 300 and we even purchased one. Through it all I was following after worldly things when I should have let go and let God rule. I must say that I loved her, but she was not my *supposed to be.*

Many times fornication is an area where people falter and this separates the person from God's blessings. As in my case, everything seemed so right in this relationship because we did not fornicate. It is true that she stressed how important it is to build a true friendship without sex. Of course, this drew me closer to her. Thereupon, we were together everyday. In any event, we did not fornicate for six months. Because of this, I surprisingly moved in with her.

I really was separating myself from God because of my life style. As a result of my convictions I asked God to deliver me from that type of lifestyle.

The devil will use his influences to show a person that a life style of fornication is okay. This is because things are seemingly done in the right way (the worldly way). Surely, this is a spirit of deception.

Yes, I was proud of being abstinent for six months, but after that I was totally out-of-order. There are many couples that are "shacking up" or living together and it seems as if they are comfortable with their lifestyle. In reality they are living a lie.

This type of lifestyle is dangerously out of God's order. It leads to eternal damnation. *James 1:15* states, *"Then the evil desire, when it has conceived, gives birth to sin, and sin, when it is fully matured, brings forth death"* (Amplified).

As men, being the covering for our wives and

mates, we should show spiritual strength. We must avoid the very appearance of evil; then our mates will respect, love, and follow the direction that we lead. Men, if your mate does not respect you for being a godly man truly living a consecrated life, and you have not married, then move on!

A woman enjoys seeing a man's strength. It is not always the man's physical strength that is important, but his spiritual strength. It encourages a woman to see her mate let go of himself and allow God to direct his path. Besides that, she knows the result will produce power of the Holy Ghost in the relationship. I failed that young lady because I did not expose her to worship, prayer, and dedication to God.

It is one thing to talk and write about these things, but it is another thing to live it. God showed me during my period of sabbatical that if I expect the blessings that comes with the desires of my heart (which was marriage), then I must let go and let God.

The things that began to happen in my life cannot be explained to one that is not spiritually discerned. God completely stopped me from all activities, including working the business that I was in. I became totally dependent on God. My fasting, prayer, and devotion time increased. Totally denying myself, I found a peace with God that I had never experienced.

Was I tempted by sex or food? The answer is absolutely yes. Without any income and being told, "Be still" seemed foolish, but to me it was not. *"Foolishness of God is wiser than man"* (*1Cor 1:25*).

When I was hungry it did not matter; I would fast. My pastor and my sister were the only persons that knew what I was going through. I will ever be grateful to them for periodically sowing seeds to me financially.

I truly believe God honored my strength because things began to happen so fast. God can move now or God can take one through a process. God took me through a process that felt like it was not a process. Often times the process is hard and long. After submitting to God, I found my best friend, spirit mate, and wife. It was supernaturally done.

The first night I talked to Precious on the phone I knew that we would have a special relationship. When I tried calling her cell and home phone, the line would ring busy. I even called my sister and told her to dial the numbers, but it was still the same results. This went on for about twenty or thirty minutes.

When I began to pray the phone lines opened up. I smile as I think about the first night we talked. There were many questions and answers. The one thing that vividly stands out in my mind is Precious asking, "Do you know how to pray?" The next thing that stands out is when we were ready to hang up she said, "Okay you can pray now."

From that point on everything moved beyond my control. The first few weeks we talked several hours per night. It was nothing to get off the phone at four or five in the morning. On the second night we talked, I remember telling her that things were not going to move in a normal time frame. In a way, she ignored the comment.

Although I saw what God was doing it was obvious to me that she was not convinced yet. The next day God really began to show her what He was about to do in our relationship.

While talking to her daughter, who she had no intention of telling about me, Precious kept asking, "How is Neal doing?" She was trying to ask how her daughter's fiancé was, but she kept repeating my name. Of course, she had to tell her about me sooner than she had planned.

Then God began confirming that I was her *supposed to be*. God showed me things about Precious that only she had discussed with God. Sometimes we would talk on the phone and she would say, "Hold on." When I questioned her about always saying "hold on," after I told her certain things, her response was, "I am talking to God about telling my business." She had to let go and let God. I think Precious was somewhat overwhelmed that God answered her prayers.

God sent Precious the husband that she always desired. During our brief courtship, I learned that a couple of her friends prophesied that she would be getting married before the year ended. They also said, " His name is Ricky;" that is my nick name!!! I was spoken into existence. Wow!!! Precious had truly trusted God and God honored her prayer request.

Prayer

Lord we thank you that you are Alpha and Omega. Yes you are truly the beginning and the end, the first and the last. I am thankful that you gave Precious to me, and you prepared me to receive her. I realize the virtue that she walks in and her love for you. I promise to let go and let you be in charge of our marriage. In Jesus name I pray. Amen.

Chapter 4

It is important to see what God sees in your mate, but it is equally important for every living being to see God.

What Does God See In Your Mate?

As I thought about what God sees in the person one chooses, I realized that I never took that into consideration in my previous relationships. At that time the most important thing was my perspective.

In my opinion, it is common practice to have self-serving standards that dictate one's attraction to another. This is wrong and usually leads to a failed or troubled situation.

Growing up I learned that a guy should not seek a certain type of girl. For example, "Do not date a girl who lives in public housing." The irony of that is my first girlfriend lived in public housing. Some people see those living in public housing as violent, struggling, poor, and uneducated.

There is a similar situation in the Gospel of John. Nathaniel asked Philip, *"Can anything good come out of Nazareth" (John 1:46)?* Nazareth was a proverbially wicked and mean place.

Many times we judge people without judging ourselves. Nathaniel asked Philip a question that he should have asked himself. Nathaniel was a Galilean and Galilee was not a favorable place either. Philip simply said, *"Come and see" (John 1:45-46).*

In order for one to see her or his mate as God sees the mate, one must agree to go beyond the natural. A person's eyes should become God's eyes; otherwise one will only see the tradition where she or he is entrapped.

God does not overlook people because of where they live, their deficiencies, income status, and appearance. Philip was trying to tell Nathaniel about a man who was the King of Kings and Lord of Lords.

It is important to see what God sees in one's mate, but it is as equally important for every living being to see God.

More importantly, seeing God illuminates a person's very existence. When getting involved with a person one may recognize certain flaws. As a matter of fact, I would recommend you not to look for them, but do not overlook them.

In the midst of seeing things in the relationship, can you see your mate searching and desiring a closer consecrated walk with God?

I marvel sometimes at the thought of how my wife looks beyond my flaws to see me the way God does. In the midst of what God saw, she met me at a time when I was searching and trying to see God.

Precious and I met at the right time. In fact, I would even say that it was in God's time. My love life had been up and down since my divorce.

A few months before Precious and I met, I

talked to God about my desires for a mate. I was searching for what I never had in a relationship. I wanted a best friend. In previous relationships I expressed my feelings and how important it was to have a best friend. In other words, I was searching for a soul mate.

After meeting Precious, she brought to my attention that "God didn't send me a soul mate, but my spirit mate." Soul mates deal with the mind, intellect, will, and emotions. A person's spirit mate is where God lives. It is where the couple lives together in righteousness, love, and oneness.

I asked God to complete my request for a mate by giving Precious as my wife. My wish for marriage was a fair request because God brought that beautiful spirit mate into my life.

Yes, the timing was right for us when we met. She saw God in me, and she also saw me in God. More importantly, the Holy Spirit confirmed this by telling me, "It is only because she sees God in you, and she sees you in God."

I also marvel at my wife's patience with me. As stated before, I know that sometimes I am unintentionally abrasive and blunt. However, I noticed that she seemingly ignores me when I act that way. Besides that, my attitude never affects her.

Furthermore, instead of reacting to me with retaliation, Precious reacts by praying for me. When I say something that offends her, I think about it instantly. Then I pray and ask God for forgiveness and I am also remorseful with her. It is one thing to desire someone who is loving, kind, and patient, but it is also overwhelming when it is genuinely given.

There are times that I feel so inadequate. It is like God showing myself through my mate. Because of this, I can see God's love, kindness, patience, and forgiveness flowing through my mate. For this reason, I strive to show myself as a better person and better mate.

I have a very close friend who is in a relationship. He really loves his mate and will do anything for her. When speaking of her, his feelings are extremely unconditional. However, their relationship is not always desirable.

Although she has some flaws, which we all do, it does not hinder his love for her. It is obvious that he sees her the way God does. We talk at times and he expresses his thoughts, fears, and feelings. Overall, his love completely overshadows his doubts.

In the beginning of this relationship they were on the same level; yet there were issues that probably hindered their growth. My friend allowed God to show him his mate. Of course, he definitely worked hard to become a better mate for her. Because of this, he could see her through the eyes of God.

While thinking about my friend's situation, I know that this would not be a workable situation for me. Yes, his mate is beautiful, nicely built, and feminine; however, the problem I perceive is she sees him with her eyes and not through God's eyes. In essence, she can not appreciate her gift from God.

God sees us, as humans, God does not look at

where we are, but what we are to become. No one is perfect and we are fooling ourselves if we think differently.

God ordains a person's mate. Many times a person will overlook the one that God has ordained, destined, and entwined for her or him. Some people often make the mistake of seeing with their natural eyes and not through their spiritual eyesight.

In the natural one looks at the shell instead of looking inside the shell. Oftentimes we become status quo in our visuals. It is easy to get turned on by material things such as, houses, nice cars, high fashion, and top paying jobs. All of these things have nothing to do with the person's heart.

It is important to seek the heart that is crying out. *"Create in me a clean heart O God; and renew a right spirit within me"* (Ps 51:10).

That is what I see in my wife. Although she is not a perfect woman, she is a godly woman. I look at her and see clearly what God sees in her. Of course, it is overwhelming being entwined with someone who has a heart after God's own heart. When I look at Precious with God's eyes the things that are minuses did not seem that great. *What does God see in your mate?*

Prayer

Thank you Lord that your eyesight is not like the eyesight of humans. You can see what we are to become and not what we are. Thank you for your mercy and grace. Let us not judge one another but walk in your judgment. I thank you that you are shaping and molding us in your image and after your likeness. In Jesus' name I pray. Amen

Chapter 5

To truly be entwined means that she is you and you are her. Your differences become likenesses.

Entwined

Understanding singleness usually involves three things that affect one's plight of singlehood. First, one must form a relationship; second companionship; third oneness. Each of these components are directly entwined with God. Therefore, being entwined with God, these components automatically fall in place.

Of course, most people want to have a loving relationship. Given that the first relationship was not between man and woman, but between God and man, it is important to have a spiritual relationship with God first. God said, *"Let us make man in our image, according to our likeness"* (Gen 1:26). Man's identity, life, and power comes from God, which reflects the Godhead. An important aspect of a couple's relationship signifies a connection or similarity between two people. Being connected in holy matrimony two becomes one. There is a spiritual need as a couple is joined together on one accord and it pleases God when God ordains the marriage.

A person's relationship also involves her or his behavior or feelings toward the mate. In fact, a person's behavior will dictate how that person treats the mate. It also affects how a couple communicates or cooperates with each other.

The Bible admonishes us to, *"Be kind to one another, tender-hearted, forgiving one another as God in Christ forgave you"* (*Eph 4:32*). Effective communication involves listening to each other's concerns then responding in a positive and productive way.

We must remember that one's character shows through her or his behavior. Surely, each person should give the same treatment that she or he wishes to receive. *"As you wish that others would do to you, do to them"* (Lk 6:32).

Another aspect of a couple's relationship should include friendship. A committed friendship requires sincerity in the relationship. True friendship has no hidden agendas or secrets. Additionally, when a friendship is genuine there are no limits in the areas of trust. In other words, life is an open book with a friend and one is not bound by the fear of her or his business being shared with others.

Being entwined emotionally in a relationship, a person shares her or his darkest secrets. Normally, walls would block these secrets, but there is freedom in this wonderfully, entwined, friendship relationship.

Precious shared a couple of things with me that she never told anyone else. She felt comfortable because I am her best friend. Friends should also feel comfortable expressing concerns without being afraid of offending each other.

When a person is in a relationship it becomes

companionship. Certainly, a companion is someone to spend time with; especially going different places. Even if Precious and I stay home and watch movies, she cuddles up with me.

I never experienced true love and companionship until God blessed me with Precious. As a case in point, watching our first Super Bowl game together was special in so many ways. Precious, once again cuddled up with me, chose her team, (the Pittsburgh Steelers) cheered and prayed for them to win.

What is more, she even asked questions about the game of football because she did not completely understand the plays of the game, nor did she have an interest in sports. Besides that, it is amazing because Precious never watches television. Nevertheless, she acted as if she enjoyed the game as much as I did. I even called my son, Jason, and we joked about Precious praying for the Steelers to win.

I thank her for showing me companionship

even when I go to Capelle, Texas on Friday nights to referee five games, my companion is right there. The gym is usually cold, but Precious sits there, wrapped in her blanket doing homework, while watching me run up and down the court. We leave home at 4:30 p.m. and return around 12:15 a.m. She never complains because she enjoys being my companion.

Relationship is oneness, it is also united in agreement or being the same. So many relationships and marriages fail because they are not on one accord. Precious and I always remind each other that we are one. I love her so immensely that I welcome the companionship and the oneness we share. I look forward to coming home or picking her up from work and seeing her beautiful smile. It is easy being one with each other because we are in oneness with God.

Reaching a place of compatibility, love, communication, trust, and commitment is a difficult task. Therefore, being entwined or unconditionally united is very important in the rise and fall of a relationship.

While being entwined a couple should crucify certain situations and relationships. About three weeks after Precious and I began talking, something happened to my cell phone. I lost all my contacts. The first thought that came to mind was, God is releasing my past associations. Furthermore, all the calls that I was receiving before I met Precious suddenly ceased. I knew then that Precious and I were truly entwined.

"Opposites attract," is a common term among physicists and romantics. Personally in a natural sense, I've been attracted to those that were more similar to me than not. There will always be some underlying factors that differentiate one's character and personality from another person. When two people have distinct differences in their personalities they should yield to each other's differences.

Many relationships rely on getting needs met

and not having enough similarities to have a stable union. Whatever the differences are each person should make sacrifices.

My son, like myself, is an avid football fan. I questioned him on how he handles being in a relationship and football? His reply was, "I told her before we began dating how much I love football."

In my opinion the startling point was, he gave her an ultimatum, either she learns to like football or they would not be dating. Consequently, she began liking football; maybe not like he does, but she watches it.

I appreciated his honesty. However, I have never been as bold and passionate as my son; I just did not date during football season, but if I were seeing someone they knew it was an important part of my life.

On one occasion my son, his girlfriend, and I went to lunch and I opened the car door for her. She immediately said, "I wish you would teach your son that." I did not think about it then, but now I wonder why she did not give him an ultimatum about football. He entwined her and she should have entwined him also.

Being truly entwined means the couple becomes one. As a result, your differences become likenesses. One may not like some of the things that the other does, but one loves to please the other. Couples should remember that no matter how much they are alike, or how well they get along, God has to be entwined into the relationship.

Many couples (married or dating), are hurting because they have not properly sought God.

When I was dating and met someone who could be a potential mate, I would ask, "Have you prayed for God to reveal your mate?" The answer was usually, "No." When God confirms and gives a person discernment about her or his mate there is a great anointing on the union.

So many relationships are dysfunctional because of attraction to status instead of attraction to each other. Some people place precedence on one's financial stability or physical statue.

Being entwined in a godly spiritual way requires a spiritual relationship with God. Unfortunately, most relationships are sexually entwined. Of course, it is okay being sexually entwined as long as God is with the couple. God is only involved when there is a holy matrimony. As mentioned earlier, ***"One should avoid fornication."***

Being entwined in a sexual way shows only conditional love. Whereas, being entwined in a godly spiritual manner shows unconditional love. Therefore, when differences occur the couple will have God in the middle holding them together.

Again, I must reiterate, having God entwined in one's marriage or relationship is the best thing for a couple throughout the relationship. Even if dating begins without God's covering it is never too late to include God.

While reflecting on past relationships I now understand what was lacking. I was totally out of the spiritual order that God required of me. It did not matter how well we got along or how much money we had. It seems as if there was always a distance when it came to our devotion to God.

When God is not first in a person's life it becomes easier to walk in carnality. In order to receive the blessings of God in a relationship and marriage one must allow God as the first love. When God is a person's first love, the thirst for God is so strong.

Moreover, worldly things and situations will not interfere and rob a person or a couple of the love of God. Do not substitute worldly things for God. After all, if God is a person's refuge and strength, the important thing is, God is that person's first love.

There are a couple of relationship situations that I would like to share that is more vivid in my mind than any others.

The first female knew my thoughts, laughed with me, and was fun being around. Of course, I had never met anyone like her. She did not like football, but she did not mind if I watched it. We were truly entwined into each other (not with God).

I was so overwhelmed by this woman, that I overlooked her issues with the church. She believed in God and I believe she loved God. She had previously worked in the church and with the youth.

Given that she had these issues she was not ready to worship or dedicate her life back to God. She also expressed the pain she was carrying from abuse, molestation, and a failed marriage. Wow, being entwined in God was the way for her deliverance.

Person number two, was genuinely kind and giving. Initially, our focus was building a friendship. This was something that I had never experienced. In the past it was all about meeting each other's needs. We were also entwined (not with God). Although she worked all the time and different shifts she took good care of me. She prayed and even read her bible at times, but we were not entwined with God. It is important for a couple to remember, being entwined is not just about the couple. The first member of the relationship is God.

If God had been the threefold cord of our relationship we could have overcome all other issues. If one is going to fall in love God's way, then God has to ordain, sanctify, and cover the relationship or marriage.

In today's society, homes are in disarray, pain, disappointment, loneliness, and suffering is in the forefront of the family unit. Husbands and wives in many homes are in great discord. Many people are doing their own thing and some couples are no longer entwined.

In addition, Satan is waiting to take control of marriages and relationships that are not entwined with God. He will try to use a man or woman to entwine in an adulterous relationship. I call them relationship predators. These predators covet what has not been ordained for them, while not caring about destroying another person's life and home.

Whenever a relationship is not entwined in God, a shipwreck is ahead. God has all power, God is omnipotent. There is nothing too hard for God. If a couple wants an entwined marriage or reconciliation, then they should give their lives and marriage to God. As a result, there is restoration for the love that initially existed and dwindled.

Prayer

Father, I pray in the name of Jesus that relationships and marriages are entwined in you. You are the author and finisher of our faith. Nothing is impossible with you. I bind adultery, fornication, abuse, alcoholism, drugs, child molestation, jealously and anger in the name of Jesus. I speak healing and deliverance over these situations. I plead the blood of Jesus over each marriage and situation. In Jesus' name I pray. Amen.

Chapter 6

People often focus too much on what they want and not what or who God wants them to have. In essence people can miss their blessing and end up in situations that God did not intend for them.

My Supposed To Be

God said that *it was "not good for man to be alone. I will make him a help meet for him"* (Gen: 2:18). Before God made this statement in chapter one of Genesis, God *"created great whales and every living creature that moved after their kind: and every winged fowl after his kind: and God saw that it was good. He blessed them saying, Be fruitful and multiply, and fill the waters in the sea, and let fowl multiply in the earth"* (Gen:1: 21-22, NKJV).

There was a reason God mated the fish, fowl, and every living creature and blessed them and told them to be fruitful and multiply. In doing so God put a whale with a whale, a bird with a bird, and a chicken with a chicken. Then God created man in God's own image and likeness. God's image is pure, righteous, and holy.

We, as humans, are God's *supposed to be.* When the Spirit of God shows in us, this means that we are truly entwined with God, Jesus, and the Holy Spirit. There is a spirit filled intimacy that one must have with God that shapes and develops one's relationship with God. Indeed, people can share this same spirit filled intimacy with their mates.

God saw that it was not *"good for man to be alone,"* after all, God created and mated every creature. Finally, it was time for man to meet his *supposed to be.* Just think about it, we as humans, are God's *supposed to be.* In the same way, God gives us our *supposed to be.* God gives a *"help meet."*

A help meet is a mate or counterpart, something or someone who serves to complete something else or to compliment. God recognizes the agony that loneliness causes even before He prepares a person's **supposed to be.** *Ecclesiastes 3:1-8 tells us, "there's a time and place for everything."* Granted, loneliness has its season and is usually a hard place, it also is a place of growth.

There are many views on loneliness and most people view it as a place of growth. I posted a couple of thoughts on my Facebook page to see the responses.

The first post was "Loneliness, is it a hard place or is it a place of growth?" Glen gave an interesting response when he said, "Always a place of growth, but never a place to be!"

I thought about Glen's response and I concluded that many go through a valley of loneliness, but stay incarcerated never being loosed from the shackles of seclusion. Some people soak in their pity parties with doubt, fear, hatred, mistrust, and all the other hindrances that keep them from growing. So many are not like Glen and do not allow loneliness to be a place of growth.

There were so many responses to, "Loneliness is a place of growth." As a case in point, D.S. responded, "Growth comes in many ways, if you are productive when you are not in a relationship you can grow. If you trust God you are never alone." I agree with D. S.. that "growth does come in many ways" and that production is important when one is alone.

The most important factor is, as children of God we are never alone. God promised us as Christians in His Word that He would never leave or forsake us (*Deut 4:31*).

G.L. gave her view from a devotional. Luke 5:16 says, "But Jesus often withdrew to lonely places and prayed." G.L. also stated, "Loneliness is definitely a place of growth. Jesus' relationship was with the masses, he preached, taught, healed, and fed them." He often withdrew to take time to be with His Father so he could re-engage. It wasn't because he was disgruntled, rejected, angry, or lonely. He simply chose to be alone. During that time he prayed just as G.L. stated; "He could re-engage."

I also posted another question about loneliness on my Facebook page. The question was, "Can loneliness be a place of happiness?" I feel that Jesus would answer that question with a loud, "yes."

According to the Scriptures, Jesus often withdrew to lonely places and prayed. As much as he loved the people he loved spending time alone with God. K. says, "We can choose to succumb to the lonely feeling or we can recognize it as our quiet place. A quiet place can be quite productive if you choose."

I really like the latter part of K's comment. When we "choose our time of loneliness" we will create quality time for ourselves. We are then in complete control of our thoughts, emotions, and attitude.

We often find ourselves alone as a result of broken relationships or friendships. No one else should decide or control one's lonely periods.

After being single for the last thirteen years, I mastered being alone. Did I grow from my periods of loneliness? I would say that I grew, not being dependent on another person's time and love that they did not have to give me.

Now being a married man, I realize that I still need some "me" time. It has nothing to do with my feelings for my wife. It is just a time to capture my thoughts, visions, and dreams. It is a time of being entwined into God and myself. We must remember that loneliness has its place, but when it is time to re-engage we must do so.

So God gave man his **supposed to be**. She did not fall out of the sky or just suddenly appeared. God said in *Gen 2:20* that *"Adam had no suitable helper."* Therefore, *"God caused man to fall into a deep sleep; God took one of Adam's ribs and made he a woman, and brought her unto the man"* (*Gen 2:22*). We must notice that Adam could not be choosy as people are in today's society.

Unfortunately, people today stereotype the woman or man that they choose. Again, Adam had no choice.

We as men are so physical and external. For example, some men usually look for a 36-24-36. I must admit that I am guilty. Some women are the same way, but more often than not, a woman is emotional and relational.

When God created the woman He brought her to the man creating instant chemistry. She had no need to ask for his credentials, nor was she concerned about physical makeup. The woman instantly loved the man right where he was.

On the social networks most men want a picture before they communicate and most women want to talk or see where the man's mind his. Then there are other women who ask about the man's occupation.

Adam did not see his mate before God gave her to him. Therefore, when Adam went into a deep sleep he had to trust God for what he was given.

When people pray for their *supposed to be,* it would only be fitting for them to trust God to confirm their decision. People often focus too much on what they want and not what or who God wants them to have.

In essence people can miss their blessing and end up in situations that God did not intend for them. Can you imagine closing your eyes, praying and God introducing you to the man or woman of your dreams? Not only do you have the person of your dreams, you are so entwined in each other and in God.

What is more, the woman came from the rib of her *supposed to be*. No doubt, there was an instant compatibility of love and a relationship.

Of course, when something is right it is like a glove that fits perfectly. After all, any other way would be uncomfortable. Indeed, every situation is different; sometimes that glove is too loose or too tight. For instance, when it is too loose there is room for much improvement. The relationship is not totally doomed, but the two parties should allow God to take control. If it is too tight usually the couple is not equally yoked.

Oftentimes people look at couples and instantly

stereotype them based on their appearance. One may see a big man with a small woman or what one considers a, "handsome man or beautiful woman" with one that is less attractive than the other, and judgment takes place. Beauty is in the eye of the beholder. What a person should really see is someone who has let go and let God direct them.

My wife says that I am "prototypical," which I do not totally disagree. There is a price to pay when discriminating against what is best for one's self as opposed to what one's flesh desires.

I must admit my selections did not always fit like a glove. Granted that the gloves were beautiful, successful, or sensual, but the fit was never right. Many times what a person wears does not fit properly. Although the apparel may not look bad, but it is just not right for that person. It is like wearing a suit that looks good, but does not look good on the person wearing it. It could be a number of things including the color, and the pattern.

When things are not working in a relationship

or marriage it causes frustration mentally and physically. Demons begin to torment the person's mind with spirits of depression, stress, suicide, and hatred. Consequently, it causes the person to lose rest or sleep because of being overwhelmed by the tormented thoughts.

When I was a senior in college, I broke up with a young lady who I dated for almost three years. I was not always faithful, but I cared for her. What is more, I was not living a Christian life during that time. Therefore, I could only care for her in a carnal (worldly) sense. Be that as it may, she never told me, but I think that our relationship ended because she knew my heart was not completely with her. She was not my *supposed to be.*

The moral of the story is, she ended the relationship and I was broken-hearted. Surely, she began dating someone else and there was nothing I could do.

At the time I was on a baseball team; I have memories of how thoughts of her would come to my mind while at home plate waiting to hit the ball. In particular, I wanted someone who no longer wanted me.

When a person is with the one God has ordained for her or him, there is a feeling of love, peace, confidence, and security.

Precious is so much my *supposed to be* that I cannot imagine being with anyone else. Who else would love me so unconditionally? As one friend said to me, "She puts up with your ways." My friend said that because I can easily be misunderstood if one does not know me. I am very direct and sometimes unintentionally piercing.

When falling in love God's way, people are in a place to receive an overflow in their relationship. For instance, God gave me more than I experienced in the world (worldly things). Indeed, my overflow included a wife who surpasses my expectations. Furthermore, God replaced my doubts and fears with trust and understanding in a woman who walks in love, prays earnestly for me, and loves me for who I am in God. Yes, it sounds too good to be true. Although it is amazing, I know it was God who provided it all.

When Precious and I discuss how unreal she is, she explains that "she was born to be married." She calls it a **"ministry of being a wife."**

I have been single so long that there is a part of my independence that stays with me. Well, this does not mix well with my wife. She gets offended if I put the food on my plate after she has prepared the meal, or if I tell her I am going to wash my clothes. I have learned to let her do her thing.

No doubt, I have come a long way since my first marriage. Being with Precious is teaching me how to become a better husband and covering. I thank God for giving me the desires of my heart. Is she perfect? That would really be mind-boggling. No she is not perfect, but a very mature Christian and wife. It is shameful the many times I failed to get it right; I thank God everyday for a second chance. I now have my *supposed to be*.

One of the reasons the title of this book is Falling In Love God's Way, is because I tried so long to do it my way and I was never with my *supposed to be*.

I was shying away from what was best for me, a woman who truly loves God. There has always been a need to have a woman who was going to compliment my calling. One who would not compromise her relationship with God, but would love her husband unconditionally with all her heart.

Prayer

God I thank you that you are my first love. You are my suppose to be. I pray that you give wisdom to all those searching for the mate that you have ordained for their lives. I pray for a discerning spirit and to be led by you. I come against every spirit of deceit in the name of Jesus. God please don't let our choices be based on superficial attributes, but let them be spiritually sound. I thank you for answering the prayers of those who are seeking to serve you in your righteousness. I also thank you for exposing your grace and mercy to those who need it. I pray this prayer in Jesus' name. Amen.

Chapter 7

When climbing the mountain of marriage one must realize that the higher the couple climbs, it seems that they will have even higher to go. The motivating factor is progression and not digression.

Don't Stop Climbing The Mountain

It is often said that marriage is difficult. Most couples who have experienced disharmony, separation, or divorce turn against the institution of marriage. I have a very good friend who has vowed that she will never remarry.

Her marriage started out great, but did not end so well. The irony is that she is a good woman and could be a great wife.

Unfortunately, there are so many men and women being bruised by bad relationships; as a result, they allow marriage to become a curse and not a blessing. I could have felt the same way.

If I had been spiritually mature as a husband my first marriage would not have failed. No doubt, this marriage ended very painfully. My wife told me she no longer loved me, even though I envisioned spending my life with her.

I grew up in a single parent home because my mom and dad separated when I was young. While I spent every weekend with my dad it was not the same as having him at home every day. There was a brief period when I remember my dad living with us. It was memorable because it seemed so right.

My mom would get up early in the morning, around 4:00 a.m. and prepare breakfast for my dad before he went to work. The time we spent together was short-lived.

I never wanted my children to experience being separated from me, because I know the feeling of growing up without a father. Therefore, being separated from my children and the woman I loved was the worst experience of my life.

In relationships people must always be mindful of exposure to character differences. It does not matter how long a couple is together there is always a learning curve. The problem that most couples encounter is that they react to the differences in the wrong way.

Just as marriage is two people becoming one it is also a ministry. Some people tend not to look at it as a ministry, and take their responsibilities for granted.

The ministry of marriage began when God presented Eve to Adam. In fact, marriage is a career; one can leave a legacy as the result of the marriage ministry. Furthermore, marriage is a union and a covenant between a man, a woman, and God. Above all, one must remember that God designed marriage.

Most Christians recite the vow that states, "What God has joined together let no man put asunder." People should reverence this sacred vow.

In my present marriage, it is a blessing being with a woman who understands marriage and its sanctity and being a loving wife.

I am still captivated by Precious' wifely attributes. She tells and shows me that her calling as a wife is genuine. She becomes perturbed when I try to do the things that she feels are her duties. For example, she does not allow me to wash my clothes or put food on my plate after she prepares meals. She makes me feel like her king.

When engaging in holy matrimony, one should realize that there will be storms. These storms come from all directions and through unexpected sources. Some storms are people who Satan uses to destroy the marriage, or those who do not understand the sacrifice involved in perfecting a marriage.

There are times when a couple will have to deny themselves for the sake of pleasing the mate. It can never be one-sided. Always remember that it is not just about one person anymore. Avoid things that only pleases one person in the marriage or relationship; be mindful that the two must truly become one and the mountain is easier to climb.

When the marriage or relationship settles or has been going on for a while, some couples become complacent. Some things they did in the beginning are not as prevalent. This is because the couple made it to a certain level on the mountain, but now staggering occurs.

I once heard someone tell a couple, "Don't stop doing what you started." Well, for one thing, if it is genuine it will come natural, and then another thing, it will be second nature. In other words, the couple should never take each other for granted. To summarize, keep the fire burning.

In chapter five we briefly mentioned the etiquette of being a gentleman by opening the door for the mate before, but never after, reaching a destination. This brings to mind, the first time Precious and I rode together. When leaving, I opened the car door for her. Once we reached our destination, she remained in the car. She politely said, "Are you going to open my door?"

Even though I stammered, "Yes," I felt awkward and thought to myself, "What?" Because of this, opening Precious' door eventually became second nature and not doing it would be totally disrespectful.

This would be the same, if she stops calling me when it is time to eat and having the food already on my plate with my water in the perfect spot, I would notice.

I have become accustomed to her asking, "Do you need anything else?" Despite replying, "I'll get it," she stops eating and gets whatever I need. She feels the same way if I do not clean the kitchen or make up the bed. Again, it is important that caring for each other in marriage becomes second nature.

There are hindrances such as, financial and social status when climbing the mountain. Worldly status does not exempt anyone from the challenges in a marriage. All the money and fame in the world is not enough to serve as a solid foundation for a blessed marriage or relationship.

Some of the unhappiest couples are successful in their profession. Fame can make one forget where she or he came from. And like fame, success can overpower one's attitude and actions. In addition, this gives the enemy another opportunity to hinder growth in the marriage. Furthermore, financial and social status, as well as fame, can cause a couple to slow down while climbing the mountain. As an example, the big "I" and little "you" syndrome. The big "I" does whatever she or he wants to. A person with this syndrome usually looks down on the "little" you spouse. This is an egocentric spouse.

The egocentric spouse can even become manipulative. There is a blessing in a marital relationship when the couple has humble spirits. The Word of God tells us, *"For everyone who exalts; himself shall be humbled, and he who humbles himself shall be exalted"* (Luke 14:11, NASB). Yes, humility is important; surely, it is a constant force while climbing the mountain.

As Precious and I began climbing our mountain of marriage, our first desire was to always be an example of a godly, model marriage. What is more, we agreed and committed that our climb would be a divine journey. Of course, we began our journey before we consummated the marriage. For this was our purpose in preparation to climb the mountain of marriage.

It is of the utmost importance to experience a period of preparation. During this time there is self-examination and then the couple examines each other. There will always be differences in personalities, but the couple minimizes differences through tolerance, commitment, and focusing on improvement.

I initially felt unworthy and even undeserving of my wife. I do not believe I was a bad person, but I know I had a challenging personality.

Precious knows how to deal with me through prayer, where others failed miserably. Precious always says, "They were not your *supposed to be.*"

In preparation for climbing my mountain with Precious, she did a couple of things that annoyed me. This is because I was not accustomed to some of her ways and actions. Over all, we teased each other sometimes and called them *"Precious moments."*

In hindsight, I realize the things that annoy me are trivial. Besides that, Precious has her own special way of expressing herself to me. Furthermore, she shows expressions of her pure innocence. I would choose her *"Precious moments"* any day as opposed to a woman's moody, controlling, selfish, and worldly attitude.

Precious' spiritual attitude gives her a heavenly altitude. She naturally orients vertically; she is always looking up. Precious does not focus too heavily on horizontal matters. Someone might say bad things about her while smiling in her face, or laughing and looking at her strangely, but she will offer her loud, Holy Ghost-filled praise and ignore the person. I truly love this woman of God. Yes, she is my ***supposed to be.*** While I was preparing to climb, Precious had already envisioned the journey.

The preparation period ends when one has bonded with the significant other. This is where components of a blessed relationship and marriage exist.

Precious and I posted a "Menu of Marriage" and a "Menu of Love" in preparation for our wedding ceremony. This was important to us because it represented the beginning of our union. Therefore, we will commemorate our union thereafter.

While carrying the menus of marriage and love the couple should discard all excess baggage. In this way, the couple is not overloaded with hindrances. Often times couples bring the residue of their past relationships into their new relationship.

If you and your mate are carrying something in the relationship that is dead or does not belong, I pray in the name of Jesus that it is removed and crucified. I plead the blood of Jesus over your relationship. Old relationships, fornication, adultery, bad attitudes, habits, covetousness, and carnality are defeated. In Jesus' name I speak love, peace, forgiveness longevity, and unity in Christ to you!

When climbing the mountain of marriage, one must realize that the higher the couple climbs, it seems that they will have even higher to go. The motivating factor is progression and not digression. We should always avoid being stagnate or not moving at all or moving backwards.

Every marriage has trials and one may stumble. Do not stop, keep climbing, never abandoning your mate. Continue grasping each other's hand, never separating from the eternal bond between you. No matter how difficult it gets, remember God's purpose and plan for your marriage.

Before Precious and I began the climb we filled our backpacks with our Menus of Marriage and Love. These menus are the structure for our marriage. The menu consists of essential ingredients; however, couples should use these ingredients only when needed.

For instance, a couple should use some of these ingredients daily, like natural vitamins and nutrients. As a result, there is nourishment of the spirit and soul. No doubt, this also quickens and entwines the soul and spirit. There are also instructions, aids, and guides included.

Let us look at the Menu of Marriage. The Holy Trinity is the first ingredient. God the Father, God the Son, and, God the Holy Spirit are three in one. They each have different functions, but the same purpose.

Prayer is the second ingredient on the list in the menu. Prayer is under the covering of the Trinity. When I met Precious it did not take long to recognize her calling as a prayer warrior and intercessor. We prayed every night before we went to bed and every morning when we woke up. Prayer is communicating with God, listening, and talking to Him.

Fasting is the third ingredient on the Menu of Marriage. It is important to have a life that includes fasting. It helps to develop spiritual and natural discipline. Fasting is abstaining from food, drink or anything that hinders a person's walk with God. Regardless of the purpose of one's fast, she or he should experience a spiritual break-through. There are times when Precious and I fast together or individually.

Studying God's Word together and individually is the fourth ingredient, and every couple should make it a priority in their marriage. The Bible tells us in *2 Tim 2:15, "Study to show ourselves approved unto God."* Studying with one's mate causes them to stay equally yoked in their understanding of God's Word.

Unconditional love is the fifth ingredient. The word "unconditional" means "with no conditions, limitations, or provisions" (Encarta Dictionary). Simply put, loving one another is based on a genuine, heart-filled love, and not what the other person has to offer.

The next ingredient, communication, is always

a necessity in any relationship. *1 Cor 15:33* states, *"Be not deceived, evil communication corrupts good manners."* It is always good being on the same page and open with each other. One should never be deceptive or hide anything from the other.

Commitment, the seventh ingredient in marriage is engaging in the vow by being responsible and loyal to your mate. The couple should take the devotion seriously. There is a commitment to God and to each other.

The couple must understand the Ministry of Marriage completely. There are countless marriages that fail because they do not understand their calling as a marriage union.

Ministry denotes that the couple is working. Climbing one's mountain of marriage is hard work. When people esteem their marriage as a ministry, they no longer act or react in a carnal way. The Ministry of Marriage empowers couples to overcome hindrances and obstacles that would normally stagnate the marriage.

Surely, faith involves having a belief. A person's faith activates her or his devotion to whatever she or he believes in.

I have faith in Precious' calling as a wife because she has faith in God. When people have faith in God, they will have faith in the spouse; they will have faith in each other and a loving marriage. As a result, one will walk in trust and not in fear. *"Now faith is the substance of things hoped for, evidence of things not seen"* (Hebrews 11:1).

There are times in the marriage when one must compromise. Compromise, the eighth ingredient, involves doing something one may not want to do. In addition, compromise is forgetting about one's self and pleasing the mate.

Furthermore, there will be times when the couple will have to deny themselves in an effort to fulfill the other's desires. Certainly, this is difficult, but necessary. Compromising is always good when it is done in God's righteousness.

Next, the Menu of Marriage must include great

romance, or an ongoing love affair. Romance, the ninth ingredient, is more gratifying than a physical love which involves love-making and feelings of adventure, excitement, and expectation. Romance involves doing things that says, "I Love You." Romance is also in the Menu of Love.

Gratified love-making is meeting the needs of one's spouse sexually. The marriage bed is undefiled. What a couple does in their bed is between them. That does not mean anal sex is acceptable. People, we must remember that the body is the temple of God. This area was not designed for sex; moreover, gratified love-making means that the couple must always consider each other's needs.

Date night helps a couple keep their ongoing love affair and not get so caught up in the cares of the world, and forget about each other.

Precious and I chose Friday night as our date night. Friday nights are strictly reserved for us, unless there is an emergency. If something interferes with our original night we change our plans. Our date night includes going out, staying home and watching a movie, or spending quality time together such as taking a walk in the park.

Encouraging each other is another item on the menu that is important. A person knows when something is bothering the spouse or when the spouse just needs uplifting. Encouragement, the tenth ingredient, is one way of showing one's mate heart-felt concern. Certainly, this is done through prayer, listening, or offering advice. Indeed, it involves being mentally and spiritually supportive.

Precious is encouraging when I am impatient. Patience is one of my biggest challenges. Exercising patience means, *"the ability to endure waiting, delay, or provocation without becoming annoyed or upset or to persevere calmly when faced with difficulties"* (Encarta Dictionary).

I am thankful for a patient wife. I am striving to improve in this area by realizing I cannot expect others to act as I do or do things my way.

The eleventh ingredient, giving, is also very important. Giving means making a present of one's self. In addition, the gift of giving requires sacrifice. As an example, Jesus was the greatest giver as demonstrated through his selfless sharing of his power to heal. His ultimate sacrifice, or gift, was giving his life. Giving of one's self means going the extra mile. It is not good to always receive. A spirit of giving should abide in every marriage.

Giving illuminates true friendship between two people. It is an unconditional bond that nourishes an atmosphere of freedom from condemnation. Best friends can talk about anything without being judged. When your spouse is your best friend, it elevates the marriage because one does not have to hide her or his feelings. Most of all, everything is given and sacrifice is shown.

I am so silly sometimes that I laugh at myself. When I met Precious, I thought she was too serious. She would repeatedly tell me that I "laughed at anything." However, there are times when we laugh together, it is fun and makes my heart feel good when she is not "too serious." All in all, my best friend understands me even when I am silly.

The Menu of Love has some of the same items as the Menu of Marriage; however, there are a few differences. Let us discuss them.

Being considerate and thoughtful in the relationship shows that the couple respects each other. For this reason it becomes easy being polite. Temperance and kindness should also be a priority. If there is a disagreement it should never be displayed in a disorderly fashion, but calmly and preferably at home.

Forgiveness among spouses is a wheel that must never stop turning. There will be times when a spouse will have to forgive and also be forgiven. Forgiveness is the act of pardoning someone for a mistake or wrong doing. Forgiveness is a synonym for apology.

Apologizing restores order. It is important to genuinely say, "I am sorry" for something that was done that was upsetting or inconvenienced someone else. I remember Precious and I having a slight disagreement over a point that I was trying to stress to her. I ended up apologizing for my actions after she brought to my attention that I was wrong.

Unusual kindness keeps people in line. There are times when individuals get upset, say ugly things, or are just not nice. These are times when one should show unusual kindness. In the Book of Acts, the natives on the Island of Malta *"showed unusual kindness;" for they kindled a fire and welcomed Paul and his crew. (Acts 28:2)*. As human beings, showing kindness, and affection to one another is very important.

Finally, there is grace *"adding elegance, beauty, or charm to something" (Encarta Dictionary)*. There are times when the husband is charming and the wife is elegant. It creates a pleasant atmosphere and warms the heart. Grace is tolerance, accommodation, and forgiveness in the relationship.

Now, the back pack has the tools needed to

complete the marital journey. One must never forget that marriage is not a vacation, but an ongoing ministry trip. Marriage is work, but the more one uses the tools the easier it becomes.

I pray in the name of Jesus for marriages all over the world; that the sanctities of marriage are reverenced with the fear of the Lord. I rebuke bitterness, indignation, wrath, rage, resentment, slander, abuse, blasphemous language, and ill will in the name of Jesus.

It is my prayer that husbands and wives are useful, helpful, kind, tender-hearted, compassionate, understanding, and forgiving of each other, readily and freely as God in Christ forgives them. I denounce the spirit of separation and divorce. I loose the stronghold and assignment that Satan has on marriages.

Satan, your power is broken and destroyed from marriages in the name of Jesus. Now climb on!

You have fallen in love God's way meaning, it was not by the flesh or through lust. It was a divine bonding ordained by God. Understanding God's love penetrates one's love with a deeper respect for God's love.

One must know herself or himself like never before. Knowing one's self allows a person to release those character flaws that would hinder her or his mate from bonding with that person. At the same time the person begins to let go and let God. Let God take control of the attitude and actions. This helps one to understand her or his mate, because then, the person looks at, *what does God see in your mate?*

Being entwined with God cannot be a missing link in a marriage or relationship. As stated before, being entwined is important because it means that the couple is knitted together in oneness. God has to be the first cord of the marriage. Being entwined is not measured by the amount of time one has known the person, but it is recognizing and receiving God's blessing and presence.

Once a person understands the need to look at

the mate with spiritual eyesight it is natural being entwined. Learning the power of being entwined with each other and with God is a break through in one's relationship. Moreover, the couple realizes that they are each other's **supposed to be;** there could never be anyone else to replace either one. This encourages a couple, *to never stop climbing the mountain.*

Prayer

Father, I thank you for being so awesome and wonderful. I thank you for being a great Father. Teach us how to trust, seek and obey you. When times get hard, let us look to the hills from whence comes our help. Our help comes from you. Lord, teach us how to endure hardships and pain. Now, Lord we thank you that nothing is too hard for You. We know our trials come to make us stronger. Even as we are climbing our mountains in life and in our marriages, we vow to take up our cross and follow You! We thank you for the victory in our relationships and marriages. In Jesus' name we pray. Amen.

Chapter 8

It is easy to have a blessed marriage when it is ordained by God. Marriage is a beautiful thing when the couple is on one accord. The man has found his good thing and the woman has received her priest, king, and husband. Each one has sought guidance and received confirmation from God about their mate. The divorce ratio would be much lower if more couples sought God for instruction concerning their relationship.

Till Death Do We Part

On February 17, 2011 my wife, best friend, and spirit mate transitioned to be with her Heavenly Father. Before her transition Precious was excited when I told her that God had instructed me to write a book about our love affair.

She was excited because she looked forward to continue sharing our Godly blessed love.

Unfortunately, Precious is not here to continue sharing. Fortunately, I have *"Precious memories"* of our love and how we always strived to have a godly marriage as a model.

While reminiscing on those "Precious memories" I am reminded of a text message that Precious sent me. The message ended with, "I love you, loving you, and I'm in love with you." After reading that message again chills went through my body.

It perpetuated two things within me, the love we had for each other and my desire to give the same to another some day.

As in my case being in love is a powerful, gratifying, and unifying experience; it causes one to gravitate to the other and when apart one is thinking about the other. In essence, while apart life seems incomplete.

"For better" represents everything good that is happening in a marriage. This is love in its purest form, which is unconditional. More importantly, love is trusting and there is no fear of jeopardizing

the marriage in any situation. In other words, there is satisfaction in the marriage and love conquers all.

In the beginning of most marriages everything seems so right and perfect. The good times are constant and seemingly never-ending.

This is the *"for better"* part of the marriage. This is the part where each spouse romances the other, looks in the eyes of the other with joy, and lives each moment with hopeful expectation. Things are going great and they are floating on air. In the *"for better"* part of the marriage, a constant pursuit of happiness is always a priority.

Furthermore, there should never be a threat of either party deviating from the person she or he was in the beginning stages of the relationship. As a result, this causes pain, disappointment, and disbelief because the person appeared one way and later changed.

Even during the *"for better"* there will be difficult times; during these times the couple must keep a sacred marriage and love each other as Christ loves the church.

An unyielding commitment to God and one's spouse is one way to sustain the marriage, while prayer and discernment is another. Through prayer God will expose anything that will hinder or damage the relationship. God also shields and protects the marriage from unnecessary pit falls. Although there are difficult times in life, as well as marriage, this is an opportunity for personal growth.

As a result of the pit falls of my first marriage, Christ became the center of my life. I became aware of how Satan's goal is to destroy any union that represents God's presence. Satan will try to influence a person to ignore the *"for worse"* vow in the marriage.

When thinking about enduring the *"for worse"* aspects of marriage, the thought of red flags comes to mind. Red flags represent negative things. Yes, one may look for red flags in the beginning stages of the relationship, but one must also be aware that red flags sometimes occur after saying, "I do."

When this happens, it eliminates the opportunity to accept or reject the relationship in its infancy. For instance, a red flag may represent a spouse who suddenly becomes unemployed and depending totally on her or his mate when it is not affordable. Furthermore, a red flag can be a promiscuous spouse, refusing to be sexually submissive, not communicating, avoiding and not spending time with the spouse, or suddenly rejecting the marriage.

Each of these situations are overwhelming. In fact, many people abandon the marriage because of the effect caused by these situations, while some marriages endure the same situation.

Personally, I realize that God will not put more on people than they can bear. This coincides with 1 Cor 10:13 which states, *"There is no temptation that is not common to everyone, but God is faithful and He will not suffer you to be tempted beyond what you can bear, but when you are tempted He will also provide a way out so that you will be able to bear it."*

Becoming disabled or caregiver for a sick family member is a *"for worse"* life situation. As disheartening as it may seem some people use these circumstances as excuses to separate or divorce their spouses. Surely, every marriage experiences trials; this is the time to unite not divide.

Additionally, there have been many marriages destroyed because of drug addition. During this time one spouse will endure stress and pain. I cannot begin to imagine what a person goes through as her or his spouse is depending on drugs.

When asked, "What should one do when involved with a drug addicted spouse?" My response is, "Pray and seek an answer from God. If God does not answer stay with your spouse until God leads you to leave. If God tells you to stay then God will put things back in order." Otherwise, reacting from emotions will cause even more damages in the marriage.

Every situation is different and to base someone on personal opinions would be futile. Be that as it may, there are certain situations when a spouse will endure this trial, while others prayerfully decide not to.

Besides that, in some marriages the spouse is physically and mentally abusive and controlling. Above all, *"for worse"* does not mean that one should allow physical or mental abuse to threaten her or his life or sanity.

Likewise, if a spouse commits adultery one should not continue to endure the spouse's life of adultery without the spouse being remorseful or delivered.

This is mental abuse and in these situations the marriage and home is in disarray. For example, the wife or the husband is suffering and the children are hurting and confused.

God is not pleased when a controlling spirit is destroying the marriage. At some point in the marriage every couple will experience spiritual warfare. One of Satan's goals is to destroy marriages; if he can do this it will destroy the family as well as damage society.

As a case in point, spiritual warfare has been a part of married life from the beginning of time; therefore, in this war it is necessary to have available weapons for defense.

Given that the world's perspective of warfare is different from the Christian's view, then the weapons are different. Specifically, the world uses weapons such as, selfishness, dishonor, evilness, boastfulness, and envy. Instead, the Christian weapons are, love, truth, hope, and patience (*see 1 Cor 13*). Furthermore, *"The weapons of our warfare are not carnal, but mighty through God to the pulling down of strong holds"* (2 Cor 10: 3-4).

Therefore, with spiritual weapons, strongholds will come down because God is in charge of the war. Moreover, Satan attacks the marriage in many ways; one of the causes of spiritual warfare in a marriage is the couple does not spend enough time together with God.

Although Satan attacks in many ways, the

Apostle Paul gives his readers a spiritual weapon, stated in *1 Cor 15:58 (NKJV), "Therefore, my beloved brethren, be ye steadfast, unmovable, always abounding in the work of the Lord, forasmuch as ye know that your labor is not in vain in the Lord."*

Looking at the *"richer or poorer"* part of the marriage vows, countless marriages are consummated as a result of being heavily influenced by a person's status. This is more prevalent now than ever before.

With the economy and unemployment continually spiraling down, these are reasons for some people to look to another for support.

In this twenty-first century it is not unusual for a person to seek someone with benefits. Benefits can be defined by an individual need. For one, such a benefit could be meeting someone who owns property or businesses, yet, to another it could be driving a luxury car, or being with someone who is financially stable. No doubt, one cannot repair or replace unconditional love with benefits.

Despite the economic crisis there are people who are still prospering; because of this they are looking for mates of equal status financially and other ways.

If I were asked, "Is anything wrong with desiring a mate of equal status?" The reply would be "no." There is nothing wrong with that because God gives people the desires of their hearts; especially, when they respect and glorify God in all of their ways. God's will is all about fulfilling the desires of the heart in every area of a person's life. In particular, *"Delight yourself in the Lord and he will give you the desires of your heart"*(Ps 34:7).

God knows a person's heart. In fact, a person's heart reflects her or his character, motivation, purpose, and goals. Therefore, a person's desires reveals who the person really is. On the whole, God has pre-ordained a person's *supposed to be*. Therefore, the determining factor is not about finances or status.

For example, it is a beautiful sight when a couple is entwined with God and each other, regardless of their status. Watching a couple hold hands while walking to the bus stop in the rain is breathtaking because it shows an expression of love and being entwined.

In the same way, an affluent couple walks into a room, one can see the glow in her eyes, while he glistens with a huge smile as he looks at her.

Thus, financial status is not important to either of these couples. It is a blessing to see moral spousal support, not because of, but in spite of.

When there is a lack of resources in the marriage the test of *"richer or poorer"* and commitment is measured. This shows that there is unconditional love in the marriage regardless of the abundance or lack. Over all, love is the main factor and it transcends physical or monetary possessions.

In our *"sickness or health"* vow, Precious and I meant every word; this is true with our entire commitment. Before her short illness and transition, Precious and I would walk every morning. One cold Monday morning, the temperature was about twenty-five degrees Fahrenheit. Precious decided to walk and I chose to stay in. As a matter of fact, she walked three miles.

The following morning Precious began to have cold symptoms. She fought this illness for the next several days. One of her symptoms included chills. For this reason, we put an electric heater in our bedroom and the room was blazing hot.

Although I had not slept in the same bed with Precious for one week, I was there to offer whatever she needed. Then Precious approached me one morning and said, "Honey you haven't slept with me for a week." My reply was, "somebody has to be able to work I can't get sick." Then she stated in such a sweet tone, "Honey, you are suppose to love me." I did love her and I wanted to reassure her that I was her *"supposed to be."*

If I had known then what I know now, I would have slept in that bed with her no matter how hot and uncomfortable it was. When I did decide to sleep with her, the bed was full of books. Although she enjoyed reading, it was out of character for her to fill the bed with books. Therefore, I decided not to disturb or sleep with her that night. I had no idea that it was her last night on this earth.

In *sickness or health* is simply saying, "I will love and serve you unconditionally." That is a powerful commitment for one to make; however, this vow is not difficult when the couple is entwined with God. Because of this, agape love has no limits in a marriage when it comes to sickness or health.

Of course, the couple is entwined with each other and God when the marriage is consummated. Hence, one will not desert the other if the mate becomes sick or disabled.

Since Precious' transition I have met several women with illnesses. Furthermore, in the beginning I would distance myself from women with health issues. Certainly, I would think about my experience with Precious' illness and death. As time has elapsed it is easier to accept these women with health issues. Surely, I have learned to trust

God for the mate and all the things that awaits me.

Growing up, my understanding of *"til death do we part"* was a way of promising a life long commitment. This was not the case with my mom and dad. I am a victim of a broken home. However, one of my most memorable thoughts as a child, before my parents separated, is my mother getting up at 4:00 a.m. preparing breakfast and lunch for my dad.

In those memories I am reminded of how it was my desire to not separate from my children and stay with their mother *til death do we part*. Unfortunately, I failed as the priest of my house, which contributed to the divorce of my children's mother. While reflecting on the failed marriage with my first wife, I realize we did not allow God as our foundation; because of this Satan had free reign over the marriage.

Speaking of priest, men are called as priest and the covering over their families. Being the priest of the household denotes being a servant, the leader showing responsibility, and making sacrifices. As the leader the priest leads by example.

In the Old Testament the priest had several responsibilities that reflected what people should do. For one thing the priest had to be undefiled. Second, he examined himself first before making sacrifices for others. This is akin to Christ making atonement for Christians through his death.

There is a need for men being pure, strong, and committed to the family. Satan will attack the head first. A priestly man will actively do everything in his power to provide, protect, and support his family.

Consequently, when a man provides he gives what it takes to eliminate any deficit in the home. Surely, a husband that is in Christ, interceding for his family, studying God's Word, and loving his family will be with his wife *til death do they part*.

Marriage represents a union, bond, an unconditional love, faithfulness, trust, submission, commitment, sacrifice and communication. In any relationship or marriage there will be challenges and obstacles to overcome.

As stated in Chapter 7, "Marriage is like climbing a mountain; the higher the couple climbs, it seems that they will have even higher to go." Marriage entails hard work, self-evaluation, and commitment. In essence the couple should take the marriage vows seriously.

I do not advocate divorce, but there are certain situations where God will be the only one to give instructions on the matter. There are marriages where a spouse threatens or endangers the life of the other spouse. In addition, many are victims of incest, abuse, and drug addiction. Who am I to instruct someone to stay in a marriage that is life threatening, being abused, or allowing their children to be molested?

Godly wisdom is awesome, it comes from above and is pure and easily being entreated. There are things that I experienced in my first marriage that could have been overcome. Total submission, forgiveness, rebuking the enemy is godly wisdom. Using this could have saved my marriage. I do remember her asking me, "What can we do to save our marriage?" Wow! What seemed so difficult then, would not be an issue now. Satan attacked us with a spirit of divisiveness and disharmony. It is important for spouses to study, fast, and pray together. There are marriages that survive catastrophic situations because they trust God and they hear from Him.

Judaism has interesting views of marriage. In particular, the Torah and the Talmud view a man without a wife, or a woman without a husband as incomplete. "Any man who has no wife lives without joy, without blessing, and without goodness" (B. Yev. 62b). The Torah is Judaism's most important text. It is composed of the Five Books of Moses and contains 613 commandments. The word Torah means to teach.

The traditional Jewish Wedding Ceremony consists of the "Ketubah" or the marriage contract.

The Ketubah explains the basic material, conjugal and moral responsibilities of the husband to his wife. It is signed by the groom as well as two witnesses and given to the bride during the wedding ceremony. It is forbidden for Jewish couples to live together without the Ketubah. If it is lost a new one must be written. The purpose of the Ketubah is to protect the woman's rights during the marriage and in case she is divorced or widowed. The husband agrees to provide food, clothing, and shelter for his wife as well as support her emotional needs. The sanctity of marriage is very important in the Jewish culture. They view marriage as being with purpose, holy, and with sanctification.

The Christian marriage also exceeds the boundaries of the earthly covenant. It serves as a link to the relationship between Christ, and His bride, the church. It is a spiritual representation of the Christian relationship with God. The Bible teaches us to enter into marriage carefully and reverently. Above all, divorce should be avoided at all cost.

There are two reasons the Bible gives for divorce, sexual immorality and abandonment by an unbeliever. Looking at *Matthew 5:32* it states, *"But I say to you that who ever divorces his wife for any reason except sexual immorality causes her to commit adultery; and whoever marries a woman who is divorced commits adultery"* (*NKJV*). The Bible also tells us, *"But if the unbeliever departs, let him depart; a brother or sister is not under bondage in such cases. But God has called us to peace"* (*1 Cor 7:15*). These Scriptures are not excuses for divorce, they are merely grounds for divorce. Let us remember that God hates divorce. No doubt, when you fall in love God's way, it will be **"till death do you part."**

Prayer

Father, I am thankful for the gift of marriage and the joy it brings. Thank you for eyes to see and ears to hear as you send husbands and wives to each other. Strengthen couples through Your Word of all you have called them to be. We are thankful for marriages being a reflection of your perfect love, which is a reminder of trust in you when we feel that we can trust no one. Thank you for granting wisdom and hope to those who are heart-broken, helpless and overwhelmed. Most of all, cause us to always treasure the relationship we share with you and with each other. In the name of Jesus. Amen.

Afterward

Precious was a wife among wives. She treated me like I was truly her king. The most astonishing thing to me was how she showed an abundance of unconditional love.

We experienced some things with each other that broke down walls and barriers that existed for years. I can truly say that this woman of God lived what she prayed and talked.

She wasn not only my wife, but my best friend, and spirit mate. As her husband, I wanted for nothing and she never complained or argued. I once asked her how she could be such a good wife and she replied that she was "called to be a wife; and one part of her ministry was being a wife."

Even when I grumbled she ignored me and said a little prayer. Her prayer and silence would cause me to come to her and repent.

As my best friend, we talked about everything; we laughed often, and cried together. As my spirit mate, we were divinely joined, inspiring to each other, and enthusiastic about the things that God was doing in our lives.

Precious' dream of us sharing our story and having a godly model marriage continues to live; not just through this book, but every time I give a testimony about her life. Moreover, this woman of God who loved me for *better or worse, richer or poorer, sickness or health, til death do we part,* inspired and helped transform many lives.

Notes

1. B. A. Robinson, Divorce and Remarriage, U. S. Divorce Rates for Various Faith Groups, Age Groups, & Geographic Areas, 20 July 2009, http://www.religioustolerance.org/chr_dira.ht...(accessed 14 April 2011).

2. Donald Hughes, quoted in Divorce and Remarriage, U. S. Divorce Rates for Various Faith Groups, Age Groups, & Geographic Areas, 20 July 2009, http://www.religioustolerance.org/chr_ dira.ht... (accessed 14 April 2011).

3. Warren W. Wiersbe, On Being A Servant Of God. (Grand Rapids: Baker Books, 2007), 32.

About the Author

A. R. Neal, known as Neal by most, started writing poetry while in elementary school. A talent he inherited from his mother Ms. Ruby Neal who is now in her 90's, and still writing poetry and inspirationals. Neal was inspired to write his first book in 2006. The title of that book is, *Am I A Man?* It is based on life lessons he learned about what it takes to be a man. This lesson occurred after experiencing a life altering divorce.

Falling In Love God's Way is Neal's second book. It is based on his spirit filled romance and marriage to Precious Bougrine Neal. His writings are very intimate and sincere. Neal is thought of by many as being humble, genuine, straightforward, loving, charismatic, chivalrous, and God fearing.

Neal is a native of Atlanta, Ga. He attended David T. Howard High School and Morehouse College. He is an ordained minister, motivational speaker, poet, and writer. He has pastored. He teaches Sunday school, Bible study, oversees men's ministry, and youth groups. He has a daughter, Maranda Neal and a son, Jason Neal. Both are college graduates.

Neal is actively involved in ministry at Destiny Tabernacle International Ministries located in Stockbridge, Ga.

www.ingramcontent.com/pod-product-compliance
Lightning Source LLC
Chambersburg PA
CBHW060326050426
42449CB00011B/2672